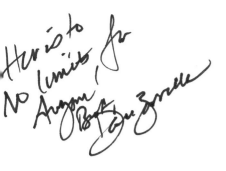

TOBY

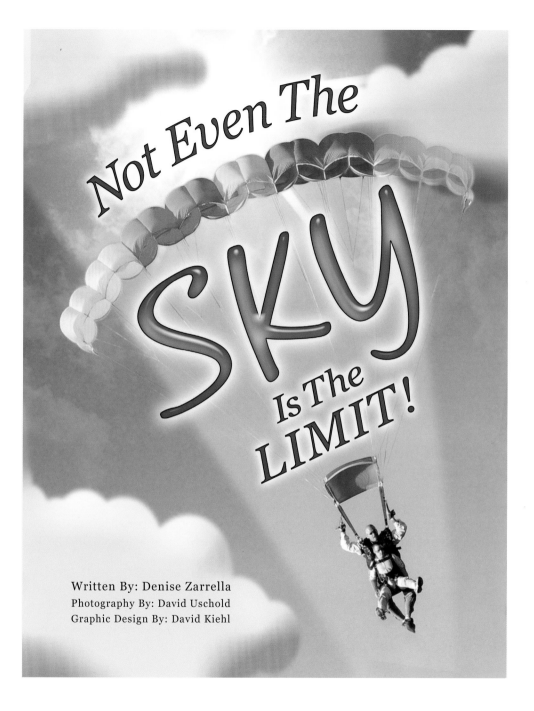

Not Even The SKY Is The LIMIT!

Written By: Denise Zarrella
Photography By: David Uschold
Graphic Design By: David Kiehl

Halo ●●●●

Publishing International

ISBN 13: 978-1-61244-199-3
Library of Congress Control Number: 2013910832

Printed in the United States of America

Halo
Publishing International
www.halopublishing.com

Published by Halo Publishing International
AP·726
P.O. Box 60326
Houston, Texas 77205
Toll Free 1-877-705-9647
www.halopublishing.com
www.holapublishing.com
e-mail: contact@halopublishing.com

This is for Gianna and Anthony, who inspired this book.

Special thanks to my husband Tony, who encouraged me to make this happen.
Thank you also to Laurie Kowalski at the Upside of Downs, Jen Judson at the
Murray Ridge School, and Julie Norris and all of the families who believed in this book
and so graciously shared their beautiful children with me and my photographer.
Also, thank you to Rodger Conley from Canton Airsports.
I would also especially like to recognize Christine Wensel at University Hospitals, who
told me and my husband that our unborn daughter would do everything any other
child does, and she was right.

LaDaja PLAYS DRESS UP!

Casey & Connor

Ride their
BIG WHEELS
together!

Ryan STACKS BLOCKS

Gianna DANCES

Austin DOES PUZZLES

Tori BAKES BROWNIES

Bobby

JUMPS REALLY HIGH

Andrew SHOWS PONIES

Anangelice

SWINGS
REALLY FAST!

Vince

PLAYS SOCCER

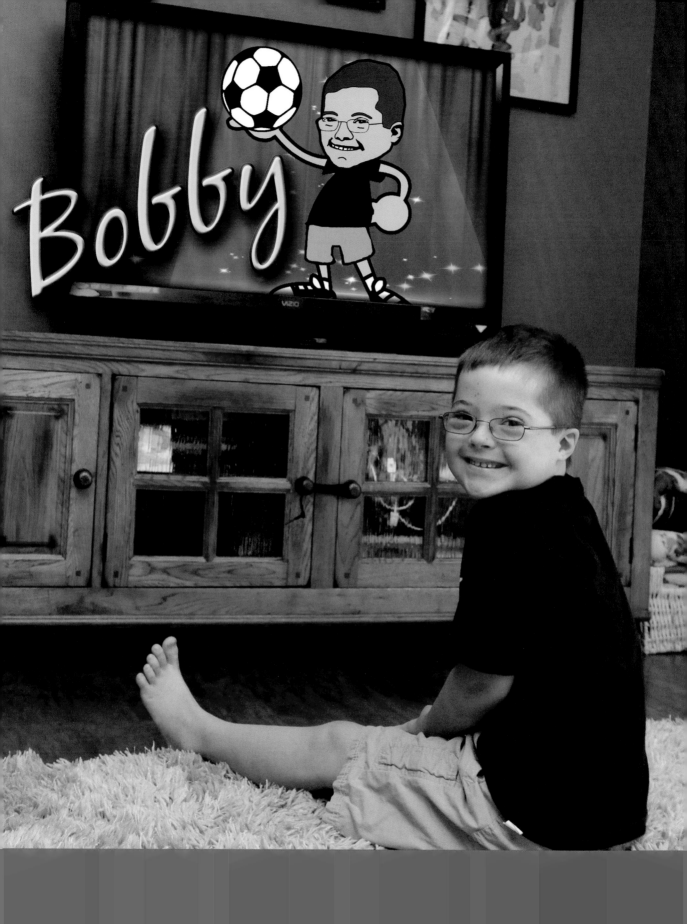

Joe PLAYS BASKETBALL

Sawyer

Knocks The Ball
Out Of The Park!

Kit

LEADS THE CHEERS!

Deja

RIDES HER BIKE

Steven

SLIDES

Theresa

SWIMS

Gus WALKS HIS DOG

Mac SPENDS HOURS ON HIS COMPUTER

Alex ACTS IN PLAYS

Ibbie GRADUATES FROM HIGH SCHOOL

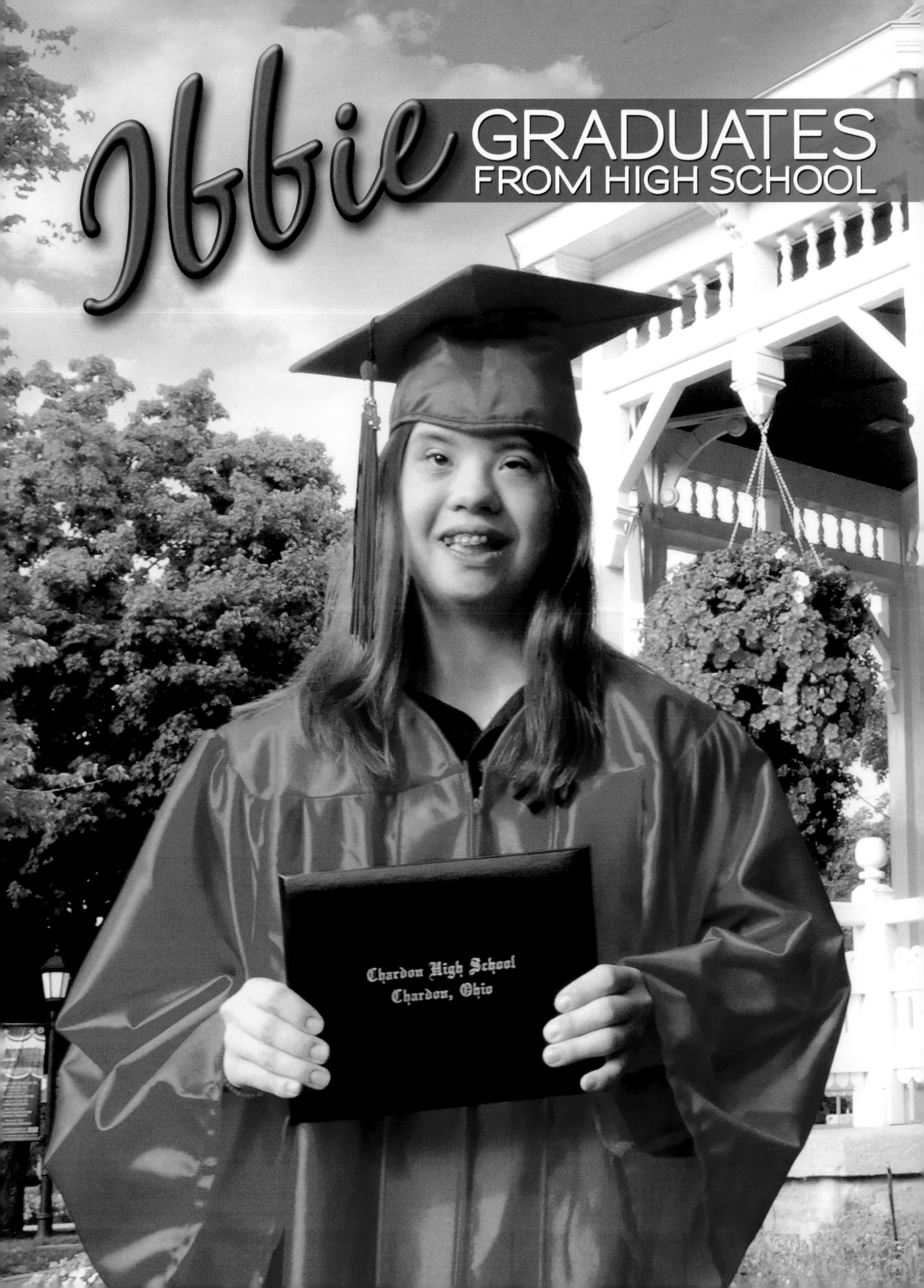

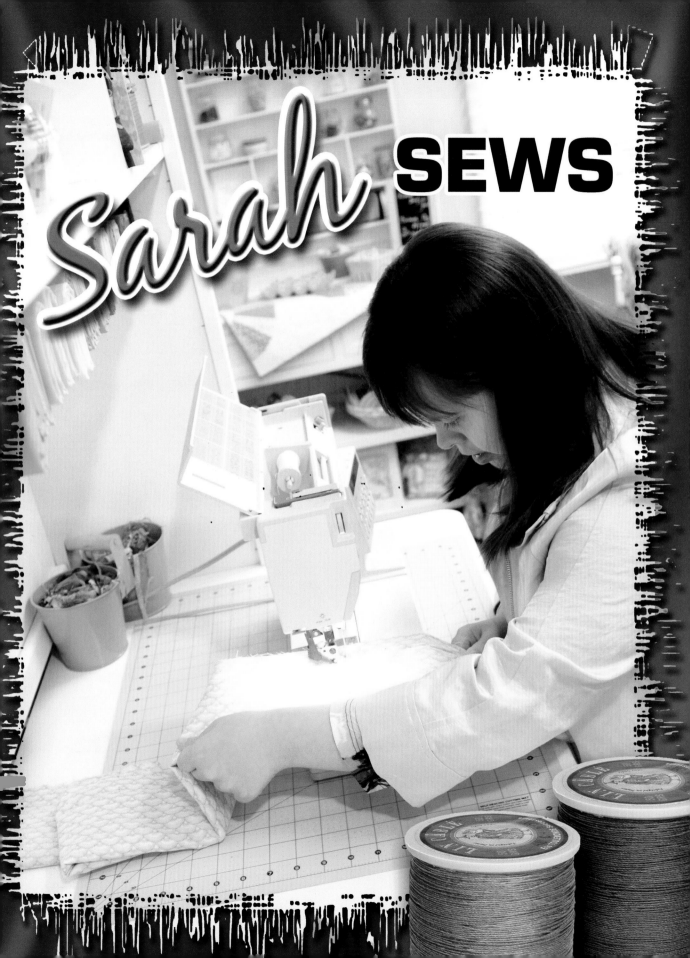

Andrew PLAYS TENNIS

John PLAYS GOLF

Toby

JUMPS
OUT OF
PLANES